Beginner's Book of Twi Phrases

Created By: KENKAN Books & More
Illustrated by: Kellie Lamoureux

ISBN: 9798796778586
© KENKAN BOOKS 2021

Samuel sits down to tie his new shoes. Sometimes shoe laces are tricky, so his kind mother offers to help him. He accepts with thanks.

Aane, mepa wo kyɛw me hia mmoa.
Yes, please, I need your help.

Yoo, mɛboa wo.
Ok, I will help you.

Samuel, yɛ akwadaa papa.
Samuel, be a good child.

Yɛbɛhyia akyire.
We shall meet later.

He says goodbye to his mother, and makes his way to his first day at his new school.

On the playground, he introduces himself to a girl named Nana Ama. They climb the monkey bars and tell each other their age.

Worekɔ he?
Where are you going?

Merekɔdware asuo.
I am going swimming.

After school, he says goodbye to his new friends and make this way to the pool for his first swimming practice.

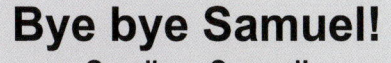

They had so much fun swimming together today that they make plans to play with each other tomorrow.

His father greets him at the door and asks him about his day. Samuel says that it was fine, and comes inside the house.

It has been a long and exciting day for Samuel. He is now ready for bed, and his parents wish him a good night

Printed in Dunstable, United Kingdom